Read All About

CATS

BENGAL CATS

LYNN M. STONE

The Rourke Corporation, Inc.
Vero Beach, Florida 32964

PHOTO CREDITS
All photos © Lynn M. Stone

ACKNOWLEDGEMENTS
The author thanks Laura Ratliff for her assistance—and her cats—in the preparation of this book.

CREATIVE SERVICES:
East Coast Studios, Merritt Island, Florida

EDITORIAL SERVICES:
Janice L. Smith for Penworthy Learning Systems

Library of Congress Cataloging-in-Publication Data

Stone, Lynn M.
    Bengal cats / by Lynn M. Stone.
        p. cm. — (Cats)
    Includes bibliographical references (p. 24) and index.
    Summary: Describes the history, characteristics, and temperament of the Bengal cat and what it is like to have one for a pet.
        ISBN 0-86593-554-8
    1. Bengal cat Juvenile literature. [1. Bengal cat. 2. Cats. 3. Pets.] I. Title.
II. Series: Stone, Lynn M.- Cats.
SF449.B45S76 1999
636.8'22—dc21
                                                    99-31230
                                                        CIP

Printed in the USA

TABLE OF CONTENTS

BENGAL CATS

Many people think they want a wild cat of some kind for a pet. Wild cats, however, are just that—wild. They don't make good pets. A wiser choice might be a Bengal cat.

Bengal cats are **domestic** (duh MESS tik), or tame, cats. But they have the colorful stripes and spots of wild cats.

Bengals are still fairly rare, but their numbers are growing. Cat **fanciers** (FAN see erz) love Bengals for their beautifully marked coats.

This Bengal cat has a colorfully striped coat, like many wild cats.

The Bengal's coat didn't come about by chance. This **breed** (BREED), or kind, of cat began with the mating of a house cat to a true wild cat, the Asian leopard cat. Scientists know the leopard cat as *Felis bengalensis*. The leopard cat earned its scientific name from its discovery in the Bay of Bengal in Asia.

Combinations of spots and stripes help give this Bengal cat the "wild" look that Bengal lovers look for.

A Bengal cat pet, like this one, should have a leopard cat ancestor no closer to it than a great-great-grandparent.

Asian leopard cats look like pint-sized leopards. Their coats are marked with stripes, solid spots, and doughnut-holed spots called rosettes. Jaguars wear rosettes, too.

Asian leopard cats live in much of Asia, including China and Malaysia. The Chinese call them money cats because their spots look like Chinese coins.

CAT BREEDS

The Bengal cat is a fairly new breed. Like all breeds of domestic animals, it has been developed by breeders. Breeders are people who select certain animals to be mated. By choosing the parents, a breeder can expect their qualities repeated in the offspring.

This Bengal cat was carefully chosen by a breeder as a good mother for the breed.

A Bengal cat breeder, for example, has an idea of what the best Bengal cat should look like. That breeder will take only the best adults of the breed to produce kittens. In time, more and more kittens fit breeders' ideas of just how a Bengal cat should look and behave.

The Bengal is one of approximately 80 breeds of cats. It is the only breed that has a wild cat as a recent **ancestor** (AN SESS TER).

These Bengal kittens are just a few days old. They weighed just three or four ounces (85-110 grams) at birth.

WHAT A BENGAL CAT LOOKS LIKE

The first thing about a Bengal cat that catches someone's eye is its coat. The coat's markings remind people of leopards, **ocelots** (AHS uh LAHTS), and clouded leopards. The coat is short, but amazingly thick and soft. Some Bengal coats even sparkle.

Gold eyes are common in Bengal cats. Cat's eyes give them a wider angle of view than humans, and they see much better in low light than humans.

Green eyes are also common in Bengals. Despite their good low light vision, cats see things in soft, rather than sharp, focus.

The Bengal's eyes are gold, green, or hazel, except in "snow" cats. The Bengal snows are white cats with dark markings and blue eyes.

Bengals have large, rounded paws and strong legs of medium length. They have medium-to-large bodies, ranging from 10 to 22 pounds (4.5-10 kilograms).

The background color for a Bengal's fur may be brown of any shade, white, or ivory. The markings may range from shades of brown or grayish-brown to nearly black. A Bengal has spots on its belly.

A Bengal has a fairly small head with short, rounded ears. Its body is long and sleek.

This blue-eyed male Bengal has a "snow" coat—white with dark markings. Bengals first appeared in cat shows in 1984. By the beginning of the 21st century, the breed still had not been accepted by all the cat breed associations.

THE HISTORY OF BENGAL CATS

The Bengal is an American breed whose history dates only to the 1970s. At that time, Dr. Willard Centerwall of the University of California began to mate Asian leopard cats with domestic cats. He was studying cat diseases.

The kittens of the domestic cat and the wild cat were hybrids—a mix of really different kinds of **felines** (FEE LINZ), or cats. Dr. Centerwall gave eight of the female hybrids to Mrs. Jean Mill. She began a program to start a new domestic breed, the Bengal.

The Abyssinian is another active, athletic, short-haired breed. It was one of the breeds used in the development of the Bengal.

Mrs. Mill mated her hybrid females to domestic males. One of the fathers was a brown spotted **tabby** (TAB ee) found in a Los Angeles cat shelter. Another was a cat found in the rhinoceros pen of the Delhi Zoo in India.

Bengals are go-go cats, always eager to explore. Their sensitive whiskers and paw pads help them get a feel for new locations, day and night.

Nearly perfect hunters, cats have better senses of smell and hearing than people. For a prowling Bengal cat, there's never a dull moment outdoors.

Over the years, Mrs. Mill combined her hybrids with other breeds, including the Abyssinian, Bombay, British shorthair, and the ocicat. From this unlikely group of cats came the Bengal.

OWNING A BENGAL

The little Asian leopard cats are great climbers and swimmers. It is no wonder that Bengal cats take after them!

Given the chance to be outdoors, a Bengal is an eager climber. And some owners have reported that their Bengals like to swim, even in bathtubs!

Bengals are generally quiet cats, but they can make a wide range of sounds.

With their short hair, Bengals need little grooming, or fur care.

Bengals are usually active cats. They love to play-hunt, run, and climb.

Owning a cat means taking care of it. Here a Bengal has its claws trimmed.

GLOSSARY

ancestor (AN SESS ter) — those in the past from whom a person or animal has descended

breed (BREED) — a particular group of domestic animals having several of the same characteristics; a kind of domestic animal within a group of many kinds, such as a *Bengal* cat or a *Persian* cat

domestic (duh MESS tik) — a type of animal that has been tamed and raised by humans for hundreds of years

fancier (FAN see er) — a person who has a particular liking for something, such as cats or a certain kind of cat

feline (FEE LIN) — any member of the cat family; a wild or domestic cat

ocelot (AHS uh LAHT) — a small wild cat found from Texas and Arizona to northern Argentina

tabby (TAB ee) — a coat color with stripes

For the athletic Bengal, every tree seems to say, "Climb me!" Cats scratch tree trunks to sharpen their claws and mark their territory.

23

INDEX

FURTHER READING

Find out more about Bengal cats and cats in general with these helpful books and information sites:

• Clutton-Brock, Juliet. *Cat.* Knopf, 1997
• Editors of Owl Magazine. *The Kids' Cat Book.* Greey de Pencier, 1990
• Evans, Mark. *ASPCA Pet Care Guide for Kids/Kittens.* Dorling Kindersley, 1992
• Scott, Carey. *Kittens.* Dorling Kindersley, 1992
• Authentic Bengal Cat Club, P.O. Box 1653, Roseburg, OR 97470
• Cat Fanciers' Association on line @ www.cfainc.org
• The International Bengal Cat Society on line @ bengalcat.com